THE ART OF FEELING SEXY

A Practical Guide for Singles and Couples

by:

AMINE SALHI

TABLE OF CONTENTS

Introduction... 1

Chapter One: Attitude and Mindset.............................. 3

Chapter Two: Form Good Habits 8

Chapter Three: Nonverbal Techniques.......................... 13

Chapter Four. Flirting Techniques............................... 18

Chapter Five: General Techniques 24

Chapter Six: Techniques for Couples 29

Chapter Seven: Solo Techniques 34

Closing Thoughts... 38

INTRODUCTION

Have you ever wanted to know the secret of feeling sexy? Sexiness is a feeling that may seem to come and go at times, but there are techniques on how to induce and maintain this feeling at will. The following guide is an exploration of these techniques, with practical advice for singles and couples alike.

Sexiness begins with having the right mindset and attitude. Sexiness is an internal state of mind, not physical attractiveness. There are many physically attractive people out there who might look like they would be a natural on the fashion runway, but that alone does not make them sexy. At the same time, there are people without model looks who simply ooze sexiness with every step they take. Anyone can feel sexy, and once this feeling emerges, others will be sure to notice. It does not matter how you look on the outside; what's important is how you feel on the inside.

If you would like to know these techniques, then by all means, keep reading. Think of this as a practical guide. We'll begin with a few techniques on forming the right attitude and mindset, and then we'll explore specific techniques you can use around others. You will learn how to flirt, how to build confidence, and how to vary your routines so you do not fall into a rut. There's something in here for everyone, whether you're active in the dating scene or you've been with your partner for years. There are even techniques for those who are single and want to remain single. Utilize the techniques that feel right for you, and you'll be feeling your sexiest self in no time at all.

CHAPTER ONE
ATTITUDE AND MINDSET

The first thing to remember is that sexiness is a mood, an attitude, a mindset. How you feel on the inside will be reflected on the outside. There's an old proverb: *As Above, As Below*. The second half of that proverb, which comes from ancient Hermetic teachings, is *As Within, So Without*. What this means is that our external reality is a reflection of our internal state of consciousness. What we feel on the inside is what we project to the outside world.

What does all of this have to do with the art of feeling sexy? It means that sexiness begins with your internal state of mind, and once you feel sexy, you will be perceived as being sexy.

And the best thing about a mindset is that it can be self-induced. You can control how you feel. It might take some work and practice, but that is what this guide is for. Let's take a look at mental techniques you can use to start getting you in the mood.

1. Take a Trip Down Memory Lane

Think of a time when someone made you angry. Maybe it was the person that cut you off when you were driving down the highway last week. Maybe it was the kid who called you names in class when you were young. Yes, we all have those experiences in our past. Now close your eyes, and imagine it. Relive that moment. Picture where you were when it happened and think about how you felt.

Take a deep breath and now think about how you feel in the present, having relived that moment in your mind. Do you feel a bit tense? Do you remember the emotions you felt at the time when someone made you angry? Are you feeling them, however slight, in the present moment after engaging in that mental exercise? Chances are your memories triggered those original emotions, and you are experiencing them slightly now.

Let's shift gears. Think about a time when you felt happy. That time when you aced a test, or the time when you got a new job offer and the future looked bright. Relive that moment in your mind. Now take a deep breath again, and notice how you feel in the present. Do you have a slight smile on your face? Did that memory make you feel warm inside?

Your memories from the past can induce emotional responses in the present. As you thought about the time you felt angry, you reproduced those emotions in the present moment. When you thought about past happiness, you were able to experience that feeling once again. That's human nature.

Let's try something else. Think about a memorable sexual experience. It doesn't matter which one; maybe it was when you were with your significant other last week, or maybe it was your first time. Choose one that was memorable, when you couldn't stop thinking about it for days afterward. Close your eyes and relive that experience. Don't rush the memory, let it come naturally, and try to remember how it felt in that moment. Remember the sensations, both internal and external. Remember where you were when it happened, remember what you were wearing or what you weren't wearing. Play it in your mind. Then open your eyes and notice how you feel in the present. Think about how it would feel to relive that experience.

See how that works? Your memories from the past can influence how you feel in the present. The first step to feeling sexy is to remember a time when you felt sexy in the past. It all begins in the mind.

2. Affirmations

Sexiness is confidence. Has there ever been a time when you felt sexy, but not confident? Most likely not. Sexiness is not the same as arousal; sexiness is a mindset, while arousal is a physical sensation. The two are often correlated, but the mindset comes first.

One way to help you develop the right mindset is through affirmations. Affirmations are a therapeutic technique that can influence your self-perception, or how you think about yourself. They can be used in various ways, but for the purpose of this discussion, we will focus on affirmations designed to boost your confidence.

The best thing about affirmations is that they are extremely easy to do, and can be done at any time, whether you are home alone, or out in public. All it takes are a few repeated phrases that you can say to yourself, mentally. The trick is repetition. Here are a few examples of affirmations you can use throughout the day to boost your confidence:

I am confident.

I am beautiful.

I am desirable.

I am successful.

I am capable.

I am unique.

I am sexy.

I am alive.

The thing with all of these affirmations is that you can say them to yourself and know them to be true. Perhaps you feel insecure at times, but the declaration of saying you are confident will make it true. Maybe there are aspects of your physical self you would like to change, but the affirmation of telling yourself you are beautiful will increase your internal beauty, which is then reflected in your external appearance. It won't magically change your figure overnight, but you will produce a beautiful smile and your eyes will sparkle. You will be motivated to start making actual changes that will produce positive changes. If you feel beautiful on the inside, you will soon begin to exhibit beauty on the outside.

The first trick with affirmations is to always begin with the phrase, *I am*, and then include a specific quality you would like to feel, such as the feeling of being beautiful, successful, or confident. Always use the present tense, so you are saying, "I am" instead of "I was" or "I want to be." Repeat these throughout the day, beginning when you wake up in the morning, and then during your drive to work, or even when you want to boost your confidence throughout the day. Repeat them before you fall asleep at night.

The second trick with affirmatios is to use repetition. They should become part of your normal thinking habits. The more you repeat these phrases to yourself, the more effective they will be. They do not require effort and can be done instantly, anywhere. You just have to remember to use them. Repeat them until they become a habit, so you engage in affirmations without needing to remind yourself.

Affirmations are not esoteric hocus-pocus. Affirmations are used frequently in therapy, informed by evidence-based psychological research. The reason they work is because when you repeat these phrases to yourself with regularity, your subconscious mind accepts these phrases as truth. And once your subconscious accepts these phrases as true, they *become* true: they become a part of how you truly see yourself.

Ever notice how the most negative people in your life are often telling themselves they lack confidence, or have a low opinion of themselves, or talk about their negative qualities more than their positive ones? What they are doing is engaging in negative affirmations: they are telling themselves they are weak, or undesirable, and their subconscious is turning these into their personal reality. The subconscious mind is the part of the mind that does not question or employ critical thinking; instead, it interprets what it receives as being truthful.

When you engage in positive affirmations, think of positive qualities, and your subconscious will accept that these qualities are part of you. However, also pay attention to negative affirmations you may be giving yourself without even realizing it. If you lack confidence and find that you are often telling yourself that you are overweight, or that you are often engaged in self-criticism, what you are doing is providing your subconscious with negative affirmations that become reflected in your mindset.

Repeat positive affirmations throughout the day, but just as importantly, recognize when you are giving yourself negative affirmations. If you find yourself engaged in negative thought patterns, observe what you are doing and change your attitude. How can this attitude be changed? It's simple: replace the negative thoughts with positive affirmations, and repeat them to yourself whenever you want to change your mood.

CHAPTER TWO
FORM GOOD HABITS

You do not need to have a perfect diet or workout five times a week in order to feel sexy. However, gorging on fast food and sitting on the couch all day is also a way to feel *un*sexy. Try to strike a balance, and recognize how your body feels, and why it feels the way it does. The trick here is to have self-awareness. Generally speaking, sexiness occurs when you are feeling your best. If you want to feel sexy all the time, or at least be able to feel sexy at will, then you will need to maintain good habits to ensure you are feeling your best.

Sleep Well: Ever notice how you feel cranky and lack energy when you fail to get enough sleep the night before? Maybe you can power through it for a day or two, but after a while, a lack of sleep will catch up with you. Make sure you get your beauty rest regularly. Take naps if you have to. Maintaining a good sleep schedule will help you feel energetic, which in turn makes you more attractive. You will be more alert and receptive to any flirting that comes your way. You will be more inclined to flirt yourself. You will be more creative, and your mood will improve overall. Yes, sleep really is that important. If you're constantly tired, you're not going to feel very sexy, so if you find that you often feel unsexy *and* tired, then a lack of sleep alone might be the problem.

Eat Well: Notice how you feel after you eat certain meals. Food can give you energy, or it can sap it away. If you eat healthy, you will feel healthy. If you are eat poorly, you will feel bad, and feeling bad is unsexy. At the same time, you do not want to avoid food entirely. You'll need your energy. Eat regularly and frequently, just eat smart. This is not a guide on how to eat healthy, but you know what that means already. Avoid fast food, sugar, and processed foods. Find a way to eat vegetables and make it a habit. Fresh is always better, but just do the best you can. And don't smoke; more often than not, smoking is a turn-off in the eyes of others.

And yes, you can cheat. You can have that doughnut or pizza. Just make that the exception rather than the norm. Balance is the key. If you cheat, don't overdo it.

Move Well: The more you move, the sexier you will feel. That's a simple but very profound truth. It's good and bad. The reason it's a good truth is because once you realize it, you will not only be sexier, you will also be happier, healthier, and more energetic. Working out produces hormones that yes, you guess it – make you sexier. When you work out, you are improving muscle tone and building confidence at the same time.

The reason it's a bad truth is because working out can be outright painful, both mentally and physically. It's not always feasible to go to the gym. If this is the case, what you want to do is to find ways to be more active in ways that are both manageable and comfortable. Baby steps are perfectly okay. Take walks regularly. Stand up and stretch from time to time. Do a round of pushups and sit-ups every day, and stick to a regular schedule. Fifty sit-ups and thirty pushups takes five minutes, literally. Do them while you're brewing your coffee in the morning. As with everything, balance is key. You don't want to overdo it to the point where you're sore and aching in the morning. Leave that kind of exercise for the bedroom. But for your regular exercise routine, think about it as a way of being active rather than trying to meet a larger health-related goal. This isn't about losing weight – it's about getting your blood flowing on a regular basis, because that will make you feel more alive.

It can be any exercise you want. If you're not sure of the type of routine that's best for you, try different ones. It doesn't have to be high impact; yoga and tai chi are also ways to get your blood flowing that won't cause you to run out of breath, and little if any equipment is necessary. Watch online videos on a variety of basic exercise routines. Don't buy expensive equipment, just find ways to move more often. Try to make it a habit. Remember, what's good for your health is generally good for your confidence and mood, and these are often precursors to feeling sexy.

Manage Stress: Whether you want to feel sexy for a special occasion or incorporate a sexy attitude as one of your established personality traits, you will first need to learn how to manage your stress. Stress is normal and everyone experiences it, but there are times when stress or anxiety can ruin the mood. In order to control these stressors, there are mental techniques you can use to ensure that the stress does not encroach upon your personal sexy time.

If you are planning a night out with your significant other or even someone new, the last thing you want is to worry about other responsibilities you may have. The solution is to simply take care of any tasks, chores, or other responsibilities you need to complete before your go out. Don't put things off for later if you're going to be worrying about them in the meantime.

However, some stressors are unavoidable. You might be stressed about things outside of your control, so it's not always as simple as taking care of all your responsibilities before an evening out on the town. To this end, you may want to explore techniques such as focus meditation, which can help you control your thought processes. If you can't control things that stress you out, the next best thing is to control your thought patterns and avoid thoughts that induce anxiety and kill the mood.

If you want to try focus meditation, follow these steps:

First, find somewhere you can relax quietly, without being disturbed, for at least ten minutes. This can be in your home, your office, or even your car.

Second, sit comfortably. You can lie down if you want to.

Third, take a deep breath, breathing in through your nose, and then hold your breath for just a second or two before releasing it through your mouth. Repeat this step several times until you fall into a rhythm of slow, deep breaths.

Fourth, recognize the thoughts fluttering through your mind. If you have any anxieties, stressors or worries, set them aside. Tell yourself you have nothing to worry about in the moment. Any problems you have are not your concern, at least for now. They will resolve themselves naturally.

Fifth, if you are planning a special occasion and that is the purpose of your meditation, imagine how it will unfold. As you imagine it, try to take a first-person perspective. See things from your own eyes, rather than seeing yourself as an actor on a screen. If you are meeting someone later, picture them, and picture yourself with them. Let the process unfold naturally. Imagine the perfect situation with that person. No one's watching; you can take it as far as you want to go.

After ten minutes, or longer if you wish, go ahead and open your eyes. You will feel relaxed and calm, but you will also feel energized. This technique is useful for more than feeling sexy, as its main goal is to reduce and manage your stress levels. But this is also the perfect launching point for feeling sexy. Try to incorporate this into your regular routine for getting ready for dates, whether it's with someone new or a significant other.

Now that you know a few mental techniques, it's time to move on and focus on communication techniques. Before moving on, just remember that sexiness is a mindset, and this mindset can be influenced at will.

CHAPTER THREE
NONVERBAL TECHNIQUES

Nothing makes you feel sexier than knowing that someone else thinks you are sexy, especially if the feeling is mutual. This chapter is dedicated to both nonverbal and verbal techniques you can use in different situations to communicate your sex appeal.

1. Form and Posture

By now you realize that sexiness and confidence go hand in hand. One way to communicate confidence is through your natural movements. If you feel confident, this will be mirrored in the way you carry yourself, but sometimes you may feel slight insecurities that will also be mirrored in your outward appearance. The best way to overcome these insecurities is to walk them off, literally.

The following technique will improve your confidence in a way that others will be sure to notice: First, stand up. Stretch. Reach for the sky, twist your hips a little, and shake out your arms. Okay, now you're ready to begin. Throw your shoulders back slightly and puff out your chest, just a tad. Don't overdo it. This works for both men and women. Keep your chin up and keep your arms at your side. Take a few steps, swinging your arms naturally. When you walk, take measured and even steps.

That's really all there is to it. That said, there are a list of postures and body movements you also want to avoid. For instance, never cross your arms if your goal is to look and feel sexy. That's why keeping your arms at your side is important. If you are someone who constantly crosses their arms, or grabs one arm with the other while standing still, you are projecting an aura of defensiveness. That's basic body language. If you stand with your shoulders slumped, you are projecting a defeatist attitude. If your feet shuffle when you walk, you will project uncertainty and indecision.

Remember, your movement is a form of nonverbal communication – you are communicating to others your internal state, often without realizing it, with every step you take. Think about all the times you've noticed how someone was feeling based on their body movements alone. Your own movements are similarly being noticed by others. If you take conscious control of your movements, you are taking control of how others perceive you. If you want to be seen as confident and attractive, then maintain good posture. Just make sure it feels natural; if your posture at any given time feels unnatural, it probably looks unnatural as well. You already know what good posture is: back straight, chin up, no slouching. The trick is to be self-aware of your posture, so you are projecting confidence, not weakness or insecurity. Sexiness is confidence, and confidence is strength. Not literal strength, but strength of mind and intention. So even if you are feeling insecure or nervous on the inside – and that's perfectly normal, we all have these feelings at times – the best way to overcome this is to project confidence through your posture and movements.

If you actively want to start taking more control of your physical movements, start by taking mental notes of your posture throughout the day. Maybe it's when you are waiting in line for your morning coffee, or sitting at a board room meeting. If you find that you are someone who often crosses their arms, or tends to slouch, or keeps eyes looking downward toward the floor, make the mental connection of what you are doing and make a concerted effort to stop. Take one deep breath and improve your posture. No, this does not mean you need to come up with your perfect sexy pose – that comes later. Just try to have good posture when you notice you do not, particularly when around someone who's attention you might want to catch. That might mean the new coworker in your office, or even your significant other. Subtle changes in your posture that really take no effort at all can have a significant impact on how you are perceived, for the better. Change your posture, and start seeing if others start treating you differently, however slight.

2. Flirty Eye Contact

Eye contact can be one of the sexiest forms of communication because it is one of the most primal. Looking someone in the eyes can produce a range of effects, so it is important to understand that how you use your eyes can communicate many different things. For the purpose of feeling sexy, there are two types of eye contact that will be discussed here: the flirty kind, and the intimate kind. Think of them as different techniques. The flirty kind is used when noticing someone for the first time across a room, for instance, or perhaps even the first date or two. The second kind is for more established relationships, when true connection starts to form.

Flirty eye contact is used to convey interest in someone. Let's say you are in a restaurant, or a bar, or the library. The specific location doesn't matter. But suddenly you see someone who grabs your interest – maybe it's someone you already know, like a crush, or maybe it's a complete stranger. That doesn't matter, as long as it's someone you find attractive. There are three steps to follow:

Look toward them, briefly, maybe a second.

Look away.

Look down.

That's it. Those three steps: look toward them, look away, look down. Then you'll repeat those same three steps after a minute.

The second time you do it, you should be able to see if they look back. If they do – and provided it's in the right context – that may be a signal of interest. If not the second time, then maybe they'll notice on the third, but that's about it. If they don't look back toward you after your third attempt, don't pursue it. But more than likely, if you are projecting your confident self and using your eyes as a means of communication, they will be likely to notice and it could escalate from there, if that's what you're hoping.

3. Intimate Eye Contact

Intimate eye contact is prolonged, which differs it from flirty eye contact. Flirty eye contact is meant to be once or twice, before initiating conversation or moving on. Intimate eye contact is the kind between lovers. It involves staring into your partner's eyes, most often during intimate moments.

When couples start dating, studies show that couples who spend more time looking into their partner's eyes will increase feelings of intimacy. This is also true for couples who have been together for a while. It's a psychological process, and it can be powerful. If that is the type of sexiness you are seeking, then practice this type. It can only be done with the consent of the other person, meaning it only works once you've established a bond with someone. In other words, this doesn't work with strangers. You should already have a read on the other person before you try this.

Intimate eye contact involves a prolonged look. Look toward them, and don't look away. It doesn't have to be too long. Five seconds is a good amount. That might seem short, but count to five in your head and imagine looking someone directly in the eye for five seconds. It can actually be quite intense.

The intensity occurs when your partner sustains eye contact and looks back. The communication is clear. And that's all you're doing – you are saying, *I desire you.* If your partner holds your look, they are saying the same to you.

Learn how to use your eyes as a form of communication.

CHAPTER FOUR
FLIRTING TECHNIQUES

Flirting is one of the great pleasures of life. Flirting is one of the best ways to challenge yourself and boost your confidence at the same time. That said, there are many different types of flirting – there's the type you do with strangers, when the purpose is simply to have fun without worrying about the follow-through; the type you do with prospective love interests as a way of conveying interest; and the type you do with your significant other or partner. Let's take a look at each of these types.

Flirting With Strangers

Flirting with strangers can be one of the most daring and exciting ways to boost your libido. Think of 'strangers' as people you encounter out in public. If it's a situation like a bar or club, then flirting is often encouraged and expected, but this can arise in other situations as well – maybe it's the cute barista, the store clerk, or even that beautiful person you see sitting across from you on the subway.

A quick word of caution, of course – use your best judgment. There's an element of daring when flirting with strangers, but make sure it's a safe situation. And also, keep in mind that flirting with strangers is not intended to lead anywhere – the thrill comes from the act of flirting itself, not the potential outcome. If they seem similarly interested, then you can perhaps escalate to the second type of flirting, when the stranger becomes someone you might actually be interested in meeting. You'll know when this stage occurs after conversation is initiated, if it's even initiated at all.

We've already gone over one technique to start flirting with strangers – eye contact. This is the best way to begin. Try to catch the other person's attention with your eyes and see if they start looking back. (If they don't, then this technique does not work). If they do, then start holding your gaze for longer periods of time. A half second, one second, maybe up to two seconds. You do not want to stare at them, of course, but repeated looks convey interest.

Once you have their attention, you'll have an opportunity for an approach. You don't always have to approach them. Sometimes getting someone to notice you is a reward unto itself. It depends on your intentions and how far you want to take it. There are also times when approaching someone else is not a good idea – you might already have a significant other, or the other person might, and your goal is not to escalate things further. That's okay too – you know your limits. But knowing that someone finds you attractive, even if it's a stranger, can be thrilling unto itself.

If you do not want to approach them, but still want to flirt, then keep it on the eye contact level but induce some self-touching. No, not *that* kind of self-touching – a more modest type. Run your fingers through your hair when making eye contact. Subtly touch the side of your arm, or make an excuse to touch your knee, as if you are scratching it slightly or pulling off a piece of lint. What you are doing is inviting the other person to look at you. Direct their eyes to where you want them to look through making small self-adjustments. Adjust your bra slightly if that's where you want them to look. For guys, maybe stretch your shoulder or arms slightly, allowing them to flex.

The thrill comes from when they actually notice you. You know that they know that you know they've been looking. Remember: make eyes, and once they notice you, produce a few provocative movements. That's all it has to be.

If you do want to approach someone, if you have already decided in your best judgment that you might want to escalate, then look for an approach. This essentially can be anything; what's important is to engage them in conversation. The most generic – but perhaps one of the most effective ways to do this – is to ask them for the time. Other approaches might be situationally dependent; for instance, if the stranger is in the same line as you while waiting for coffee, ask them for a recommendation. If it's someone in class, ask them if they wrote down the assignment because you conveniently forgot.

Based on their response, the conversation will either continue or end. If they provide a simple response and do not seem interested in continuing, then that's okay – you tried your best. But if they are interested and available, however slight, the conversation might continue. If that is your goal, then let it continue.

Remember, the goal with flirting with strangers is not to escalate the situation; instead, it's to provide you with that boost of self-confidence you get when you know that you've been noticed. Sometimes it does escalate if that's what both people want, but that is not the primary goal of this type of flirting. That's why it doesn't matter if it never leads anywhere.

Flirting with a Prospective Interest

This method of flirting is for those with whom you've already developed a rapport – in other words, people you know, even if you haven't elevated to the next step. This method includes everything from the Flirting with Strangers section, but builds beyond this. This is the type that involves direct communication, or words.

There are many different things to include, as any conversation you initiate with this person will depend on the situation at hand. Speaking with a friend (a cute friend) is different than speaking with a coworker. However, the commonality in all situations is that you want to find subtle ways to demonstrate your interest, and also to find ways to boost their own confidence at the same time. This is because of the rule of reciprocity in conversations – say something nice and the other person will feel compelled to say something nice in return. Let's go over a few examples.

First, you want to plan ahead. Your goal here is to find a way to compliment them, and you want to have this ready before starting to speak with them. Take a moment before approaching to look at them. Is there anything unique or different about their appearance? Are they wearing their hair a new way, are they wearing a new pair of shoes? It doesn't matter too much – simply pick a detail about their appearance and make a mental note.

Second, when speaking with this person, maintain eye contact. You often want to initiate the communication by discussing something *other* than your intent. If it's at work, make it about work. If it's an acquaintance or cute friend, you can start with something innocuous, such as asking about their latest weekend. Speak with them as you normally would, but at a key moment in the conversation, find a way to drop the compliment about the thing you noticed. It can be a random shift in the conversation – maybe during a natural lull in the conversation, when you can tell them you like their hair, their outfit, even their perfume or cologne. This might catch them off guard, but that's a good thing – these are the types of moments that make a conversation memorable, and you want them to remember you. Their initial reaction, especially if they are a bit surprised, might be to simply thank you for the compliment. At this point, flash them a smile. What you do next depends on their reaction: if they compliment you back, then you can continue the conversation from there. If they are uncertain how to lead the conversation, that's okay too – flash them that smile, look them in the eye, and tell them you'll see them later and end the conversation. That's it.

Simple, right? The goal here is not to escalate in the moment, but rather to lay the foundation for subsequent flirting down the road. They will have noticed you, and they will have read your interest, at least subconsciously, and that should be your goal in this particular situation. You will feel more confident and daring for having initiated the flirtation, and in doing so, you will have laid the foundation for escalating the relationship if you desire. You never actually have to escalate the relationship if you decide you don't want to. Sometimes it's simply okay to build a bit of sexual tension, which is what you are doing. At the very worst, you will be able to read if they are interested or not – if they are not, that's perfectly okay too. Pursuing someone who is unavailable or uninterested is not a sexy feeling, so at the very least, you'll have an understanding that you should direct your attention elsewhere.

Flirting With Your Partner

Flirting with your partner is a way to keep the spice alive in a relationship. After the honeymoon phase, couples tend to fall into patterns, and sometimes this can reduce the amount of romance and desire. You don't want to fall into this routine, so there are several ways to flirt within a relationship that will keep the sexual energy alive.

First, focus on intimate eye contact. Remember, prolonged looks during opportune moments.

Second, don't stop complimenting someone on their appearance just because you've gotten close with them. Compliments are a continual confidence-booster, and making the other person feel confident will result in them making similar compliments toward you – that's how the rule of reciprocity works, and it's something we've all been socially ingrained with.

Third, be direct. If your goal is to have a sexy and intimate evening, then initiate it in the morning by being direct with your partner. Tell them you want them, you desire them, right before one of you leaves for work. That will keep their thoughts on you throughout the day, building sexual tension for you and them.

Fourth, send them random messages that communicate something sexual. Refer to past times when you were intimate. If you're feeling daring, send them a provocative selfie. Your goal is to continuously reaffirm your sexuality, and this is important to keep the relationship from falling into routine. Look for ways to communicate sexual desire, and this will naturally increase sexual tension. It doesn't require anything overt or expensive; instead, all it requires is that you be direct in what you want and how you feel. Take the lead – sometimes your partner my feel inhibited or not overly open to forms of sexual communication, and that goes for both men and women. If you take the lead, however, you are establishing a framework for your relationship that regularly incorporates an element of sexuality that is important.

Similar to how your actions will have an effect on your partner, engaging in this type of flirtation will also have an effect on yourself – by communicating sexual desire, you are increasing your own natural flow of sexual energy, and this is sure to increase your own feelings of sexiness throughout the day.

CHAPTER FIVE
GENERAL TECHNIQUES

The following techniques are general tips that apply to everyone, including men, women, singles and couples. This is not a checklist; simply find the tips that work for you, and you will be your sexiest self in no time.

1.Change Your Appearance

No, this doesn't have to mean anything drastic. Instead, look for little ways you can change your look. Wear your hair in a different style. When you wear a new look, others will be sure to notice. Visit a salon or barber and try something different, perhaps that look you've always wanted to try but never did. If you do not want to alter your current hairstyle, then perhaps wear your hair down if you usually wear it up, or vice versa.

For guys, try growing a five o'clock shadow, or shave if you normally wear a beard. For ladies, try a different shade of lipstick or new makeup routine. Dye your hair a different shade.

There are many subtle ways you can alter your appearance. When you go out in public, people you normally encounter throughout your normal routines will most likely notice something is different about the way you look – including your significant other, or perhaps your office crush. Once people start to notice, you'll notice the additional attention, and this is one way to boost your confidence.

2.Change Your Routine

Know what's sexy? Excitement. We often establish routines for ourselves that become monotonous, and monotony is rarely associated with sexiness because monotony is boring. If you want to get the blood flowing, one thing to do is to change your routine and be a bit daring. Maybe this involves taking that trip you've always wanted, or perhaps it involves signing up for dance lessons. In fact, there are many ways to induce excitement into your life, whether big or small.

Make a list of activities you've always wanted to try. Challenge yourself if you feel hesitant about trying new things. It's okay if you feel that way – the important thing is to actually write down things you want to try. It's up to you what you find exciting, so there are a million different activities this could be. It could be as simple as visiting that new restaurant that opened down the street, or it can involve finally going on that cruise you've always considered. For couples, this also allows a chance to bond and build intimacy, while for singles, it provides new opportunities to meet people.

Staying at home in a rut is rarely sexy; going out and doing something new can be exciting, and this excitement will also make you feel sexy on the inside.

3.Body Tip: Speed Things Up

Physical activity can be invigorating, and this can induce feelings of sexiness. While we've already discussed working out as one way to increase your physical activity, it's not the only way.

Take opportunities to walk when you might normally drive. Go for walks at random, either with your significant other, or if you're single, walking alone is fine too. You want to get your blood flowing, in the literal sense, and this will make you feel better and healthier overall. While a regular workout schedule is always recommended, if you find you do not have time, find little ways you can increase your amount of physical activity throughout the day.

Feeling fit and active is one of the best ways to increase your libido. Even if what you're doing is not working out per se, the simple action of increasing your blood flow is a precursor to getting you in the mood.

4. Body Tip: Slow Things Down

Feeling invigorated is one way to feel sexy, but afterward, there is value in pampering yourself. Nothing beats a long workout followed by a hot bath, where you can relax in the tub with a bath bomb. Soothe your muscles with a gentle massage. Rub your neck and your shoulders with a massage oil. If you have someone to do this for you, all the better, but you can also do this on your own, either with your own hands or a massager. As you do, take deep slow breaths, and throw in a few affirmations as well. See where things lead. If with your significant other, this is often one of the quickest ways to induce intimacy. If you are alone, this could make you want to spend a little quality time with yourself. No one's watching, it's okay.

Sexiness is a mental mindset, so by slowing things down, you are calming yourself and inducing a deep state of relaxation that can recharge and increase your natural libido.

5.Clean Your Home

Giving your home a thorough cleaning might not be the first thing that comes to mind when you think of a sexy activity; however, if you have a clean and organized living space, it's much easier to feel sexy than if you have a sink overflowing with dirty dishes, mounds of dirty laundry, and kitty litter tracked all over your home. Even knowing you have all these chores to do can be a mood-killer. Even if you share your space with a significant other, a cluttered and messy home might be killing the mood for both of you. Notice how you always feel more relaxed and calm when the house is spotless, and all the annoying chores of daily life have been checked off your list? The first thing you will feel is accomplishment, and then you'll feel relaxed. And this relaxed feeling is always one of the best precursors to sexiness. Getting all of your chores done can also be a way to build confidence, however slight. Look for little ways to free your mental space by clearing out your physical space.

Think of this as more of a tip on how to not feel *un*sexy. Spend some time cleaning your space, and you'll feel more relaxed over-all – and feeling relaxed is one of the best ways to start feeling sexy overall.

6.Create Ambience

Whether solo or with a partner, setting the ambience of your space is one of the keys to feeling sexy. Light some candles or burn some incense. Lower the lights – lighting is important when establishing mood, so invest in a dimmable light, or find a lamp you can strategically place to provide some light, but not too much. Create a playlist of your favorite mood-setting music, whether it's slow jazz, trance beats, or even classical. A little creativity can transform your space, creating the right amount of ambience for your sexy mood.

7.Go Shopping

Similar to changing your look in little ways, such as wearing a new shade of lipstick or sporting a different hairstyle, finding a few new items to add to your wardrobe can be a way to complete a sexy makeover. Find items that flatter your appearance. Wear a different style bra, splurge on a new skirt, or even a new pair of pumps.

The trick here is to find clothes that will boost your confidence, for guys as well as the ladies. And if you want to spice things up, buy some new lingerie. Even if you're single, wearing something enticing beneath your outer clothes will help you maintain that feeling of sexiness throughout the day. No one has to know but you.

CHAPTER SIX
TECHNIQUES FOR COUPLES

The following are a variety of activities you can engage in with your partner to elevate the sexual energy between you. These can help ensure that you maintain an active and healthy sexual relationship over time. Read through the following and try to ones that sound most appealing. Here, the trick is to incorporate some of these activities on a regular basis, so they become a normal part of your relationship.

1.Hold Hands

Yes, this one is very simple but it's also very effective. When you are out with your partner, hold hands when you walk. Maybe not all the time, but enough for it to be a regular thing. If you want to include an element of seduction, don't just hold your partner's hand – play with it. Stroke his or her fingers, slowly. Rub the back of their hand with a fingertip. All of this can be subtle; it's like playing footsie but you're using hands instead, and it can be done in public. This is a powerful form of communication that conveys to your partner both your affection and desire. It can be done anytime, anywhere.

2.Announce Your Intentions

Once you have developed a level of intimacy with your partner, take advantage of that intimacy by allowing yourself to be uninhibited about what you want and what you desire. Use this as a way to increase sexual tension. This is similar to the discussion on flirting with your partner, but if you want to escalate it a notch, tell your partner *exactly* what you want to do with them. Don't be inhibited – be forward and direct.

If you want to use this technique to maximize sexual tension (ensuring that the intimacy that follows will be intense), tell this to your partner when the two of you are out in public. Maybe the two of you are out shopping, or it's the beginning of a date before the two of you head out. It might even be a dinner party when the two of you are out with a group of friends. Simply lean in close to your partner – you want to keep it private, after all – and tell them exactly what you want to do with them the moment you two are home alone. Be specific, and if you want to kick it up a notch, describe it as well. You want your partner to picture it in his or her mind, and from this point, the two of you will be in a state of desire for the rest of the evening. Let your partner know you aren't shy, at least not with them. The language you use doesn't have to be modest or polite – sometimes being direct and explicit can produce the most desirable effects.

3.Vary Your Intimacy Routine

If you've been with someone a while, most likely you've fallen into certain patterns. This is a good thing, as patterns help create stability in a relationship. However, you want to avoid your intimacy and lovemaking becoming too formulaic. Maybe you have that three times a week schedule, after the lights are out and the two of you are lying in bed. This can make sex start feeling routine, and while this might keep you feeling sexy during those intimate moments, varying your schedule can increase feelings of sexiness that do not fall into a routine.

There are two ways to vary your routine: either time of day, or location. This works for any couple, whether you're still in your first few months or have been together for decades. Varying the time of day is self-explanatory, but you might be the one who needs to initiate it if your partner isn't expecting it. Simply initiate by touching your partner and time when he or she isn't expecting it. Maybe surprise them the instant they walk through the door, signaling your intention by wearing something provoking. If your normal time for intimacy is at night, try touching them in the morning or the afternoon. Find a time when you can surprise your partner, when they are least expecting it.

Similarly, look for ways to vary where your intimacy occurs. It doesn't always need to be the bedroom. If the two of you are on the couch, stay on the couch. If it's when one of you is doing dishes, use the kitchen counter if it's feasible to do so. If you want to be daring, go for a drive with your partner. Find a secluded place, and find ways to be intimate while out and about. Use your best judgment, of course; however, if you are looking for an additional thrill and variation to your normal routine, finding new locations can be an effective way to remain creative and playful when being intimate with your partner.

Over time, these 'special occasions' will become part of your new routine, and this is the type of routine you want to have – one that's unpredictable, so it always keeps you and your partner's mind on the thought of intimacy.

4.Share Fantasies

Fantasies are normal and healthy, even if they feel taboo. Sharing your fantasies with your partner can be one of the best ways to spark creativity and desire in the bedroom. If this is something you and your partner are not used to doing, you will have to be the one to initiate it. Your partner might feel hesitant at first, particularly if you ask them to share a fantasy with you without sharing one first.

If you're feeling bold, however, start by sharing one of your fantasies first. You can start off tame, and gauge your partner's reaction. If they're into it, then go ahead and share a little more. Throw in an expletive or two. Be as revealing as you want. The simple act of sharing your most private thoughts can be thrilling, and this thrill will only increase once you see the reaction it has on your partner. Tell them while you're being intimate. Speak into their ear. This will help you push boundaries and it will provide you opportunities to explore new elements in your lovemaking.

Words alone can have a powerful seductive impact. If you want to feel sexy, use words to put yourself and your loved one in the mood, then keep using your words to escalate from there.

5.An Intimate Photoshoot

Boudoir photography is one way to spice up intimacy between couples, but you don't always need to hire a professional photographer. If you're feeling a bit daring, try incorporating suggestive photography. You can use it as a way to tease your partner, such as sending a selfie when you're away, or you can use it more directly and intimately during your most private moments. Take turns taking photos of one another in provocative poses. Just the act of posing or viewing someone through a lens can produce feelings of excitement, and it can dramatically escalate the sexual tension within the room.

Naturally, there may also be a concern with privacy. To this end, there's no need to actually keep the photos once they've been taken. Remember, it's the act of taking the photos that can produce that titillating impact, so if long-term privacy is your concern or you don't want to risk keeping or sending intimate photos, simply delete them once they've been taken. If you want to guarantee the images will be wiped, have them taken on your own phone, and then you'll be the one to delete them afterwards.

6. Role Play

One of the best ways of overcoming inhibitions is to role play. Assume a role that you and your partner find appealing, and inhabit that role. Think of yourself as a character, rather than yourself, and have your partner do the same. It can be as cliché as playing doctor, or perhaps something more creative. The reason this is effective is because many of the barriers to intimacy are a result of personal inhibition. However, when you assume a different role, you can create your own character. It's not you – it's a character you've created, one with his or her own independent fantasies that you can explore and express. There are many different roles you can try, so this is one way to make sure that your encounters can keep feeling new and exciting.

CHAPTER SEVEN
SOLO TECHNIQUES

Maybe you're reading this guide because you're single, and looking for ways to improve your sexiness to attract a partner. Maybe you simply prefer being single. That's normal and healthy and good, but it doesn't have to mean you can't express or explore your sexuality just because you're solo. Let's look at a few techniques you can use to increase your libido, even if you don't currently have a partner.

1.Find an Online Community

The best thing about online interactions is that you can remain anonymous. There are many adult-themed networks out there, such as on Reddit or other social media sites. We're not talking about hookup sites here – those are perfectly fine to explore as well if that is what you are seeking, but there are also sites where people can engage in discussions about a variety of sexually-themed subjects. Simply the act of reading the thoughts of others can be a way to increase your libido in the moment.

Better yet, find an online partner where you can share whatever you want with them without fear of feeling judged. Sharing fantasies with a stranger can be exciting, and you don't have to worry about revealing too much because it simply doesn't matter. Just a word of caution – keep it anonymous, and don't share anything *too* personal, like details about your life. You don't have to send a photo, and you probably shouldn't, unless you get to the point where you feel like you can trust them a little more.

If your goal is to simply remain anonymous, however, finding someone online who might be into the same thing can be one way to maintain your libido even when you're single.

2.Get Out

Remember when we discussed how to flirt with strangers? If you want to maintain feelings of sexiness while single, find ways to subtly flirt when you are out and about. If you're no opposed to heading to a local bar or club to try this out, then by all means, get out there and get your flirt on. However, it doesn't have to be limited to those types of environments. One of the best ways to build confidence, even while single, is knowing when someone finds you attractive. It can be virtually anywhere – the grocery store, the post office, anywhere you stumble across someone you find attractive. Look people in the eye. Smile when you talk. You don't have to think of it as flirting, and you don't need to necessarily try to flirt with everyone you see. Think of it as being nice and friendly. Engage people in conversation when given the opportunity. Don't wait for people to start talking to you; instead, be the one who initiates the conversation.

Once people recognize you're willing to engage with them, you'll be able to read their signals more clearly, and that will let you know whether you want to escalate to flirting, or simply move on. All that matters is that you generate some sort of positive response; it doesn't need to be flirtatious or romantic, just positive. This will help boost your confidence and confidence alone can help you feel sexy.

3.Reconnect

Even if you don't have someone special in your current life, you most likely have people in your past. While it might not be the best to contact one of your exes, you more than likely have people in your past that almost connected with, but never truly did. Take the time to find someone you might want to reconnect with and shoot them a text or an email, just to say hi. No, it doesn't need to be laden with sexual innuendo, and it's probably best if it doesn't – at first. However, the simple act of reconnecting with someone from your past can build your confidence, especially if you find that too much of your time is being spent alone. Think of it as a way to keep being social. If they respond and want to continue the conversation, you can start to incorporate some of the flirting techniques you learned earlier. If the conversation is conducted entirely over text or email, then you won't have the ability to utilize your eye contact techniques, but you can still find ways to compliment the other person. As with most situations involving social interactions, you always want to have a read on the other person. But even if it never amounts to flirting, the simple act alone of communicating with someone from your past can be a way to make you feel more confident, and as we've seen already, confidence is the best way to boost your overall sex appeal.

4. Break All the Rules – No One's Watching

As you've read through this guide, you've noticed several recommendations you should follow if you want to feel sexy – eat healthy, keep your space clean, try to be active. These are all well and good, but if your plan is to have some self-indulgent solo time, then make it as indulgent as you possibly can for an evening. Go ahead and buy that gallon of ice cream, lounge around in your favorite sweatpants, and indulge in a Netflix marathon. Maybe find something enticing. Tell yourself that all you want to do for an evening is to feel as good as you possibly can. Use this as an opportunity to indulge completely in yourself. Take a hot bath, and don't bother getting dressed afterward. Light some candles, burn some incense, turn off your phone and spend some quality time with yourself. Don't rush it – prolong it for a while. Use this as an opportunity for some solo self-exploration.

Closing Thoughts

Sexiness is a mood, a mindset, an attitude. Sexiness is not about achieving a certain figure; sexy exists at any size. If you adopt the attitude that sexiness is a mindset, the first thing you will realize is that a mindset can be influenced at will. As you start to incorporate some of the techniques you've learned in this guide, remember that anyone can be sexy – all it takes is the right attitude, and yes, you can consciously control your attitude and outlook.

You will most likely find some of these techniques to be more effective than others. We all have our own individual buttons that we prefer more than others. Just use the ones that seem right for you. If you ever feel uncomfortable with any of these techniques, simply try another.

What each of the techniques presented in this guide have in common, however, is they are all designed to help boost your individual confidence. Confidence is sexy; we've all heard that before, including in this guide, but it is important to take it to heart. Confidence can only be manifested from within; it cannot be faked. Instead, confidence comes from self-awareness and overcoming challenge. When you form good habits, your confidence will be boosted from feeling healthy and fit. When you flirt, the affirmation you will get from being noticed will increase your confidence naturally as well.

Have the confidence to know that everyone has a sexual side. Have the self-awareness to accept your own sexual nature, and don't be afraid to explore it. Self-awareness and confidence will strengthen your relationship if you have a significant other, and it will keep your relationship from falling into a routine. If you are single, self-awareness and confidence will give you the boost you need to approach others and it will improve how you are perceived by others. You will be more memorable and more attractive, and knowing someone else finds you attractive is one of the most effective ways of making you feel desired.

The best part about building confidence is that it becomes its own reward. If you are able to flirt successfully once, you will have the courage to do it again. All of these techniques will become easier over time, even the hard ones, such as maintaining a regular exercise or workout routine. Your confidence will grow with each success, and you will be able to transform your overall attitude and mindset in ways that will improve many different aspects of your life, not just your sexuality.

If you are ever feeling unsexy or feel like you are in a rut, remember that you can induce a feeling of sexiness through thought and memory alone. As Within, So Without. It all begins in the mind. You can use mental techniques, such as focus meditation, to put you in a more relaxed and responsive mood. Use affirmations as a way to boost your internal confidence. Learn to use your eyes. Flirt when you have the opportunity to do so. Maintain good habits and good health. Communicate with your partner. Use variety. Challenge yourself and be daring. If you follow one or all of these recommendations, you will be sure to increase your feelings of sexiness and you will have more control over your sexuality.